A Weekly Reader Exclusive

GREMLiNS

This book is a presentation of Weekly Reader Books. Weekly Reader Books offers book clubs for children from preschool through junior high school. For further information write to: Weekly Reader Books
1250 Fairwood Avenue
Columbus, Ohio 43216

Weekly Reader Books offers several exciting card and activity programs. For information, write to WEEKLY READER BOOKS, P.O. Box 16636, Columbus, Ohio 43216.

Published for Weekly Reader Books by arrangement with Western Publishing Company, Inc.

by Michael Teitelbaum
illustrated by Luis Dominguez

A GOLDEN BOOK • NEW YORK
Western Publishing Company, Inc., Racine, Wisconsin 53404

Billy Peltzer and Kate Beringer were friends. Gizmo was Billy's pet. Billy's Dad had given him the unusual creature as a Christmas present.

All three stared in horror at the destruction going on around them.

There were gremlins everywhere. Hundreds of the vicious, ugly creatures were running through the town, terrorizing people and destroying property.

One gremlin tossed a rock through a store window.

Another gremlin was hiding in a mailbox. When Billy's neighbor went to mail his Christmas cards, the gremlin pulled him in.

Two more captured a little girl's puppy, and carried him away.

The gremlins weren't afraid of anything—except bright light. They knew that bright light would kill them. As the sun began to rise, all the gremlins ran in terror. They needed to get out of the sunlight and into a dark, safe place.

Billy set off an explosion in the movie theater. "We did it!" he cried. "We destroyed all the gremlins!"

"What a relief," said Kate.

Suddenly Gizmo screamed and pointed at something across the street.

"What's wrong, Gizmo?" Billy asked.

Oh, no!

Stripe, the leader of the gremlins, had managed to escape the explosion.

Stripe ran into a department store. It was dark inside, and it would be easy for him to hide in such a large store.

Billy, Kate, and Gizmo followed him in.

You and Gizmo try to find the lights. I'm going after Stripe!

Billy cautiously made his way up and down the aisles of the store. There was no sign of Stripe.

When he reached the toy section, Billy heard a noise.

What's that?

Dozens of wind-up toys were moving along the floor. For a moment, Billy felt relieved. Then he heard a strange giggle.

For Christmas, Billy Peltzer's father wanted to give his son something special. That's how it all began, with the very unusual present wrapped up inside that box.

Special Bonus Photo Section With Scenes From The Movie

Billy gives his cute, playful little pet a name: Gizmo. He's so delighted, he even lets the Mogwai sleep in his bed.

In the bank where Billy is employed, Mrs. Deagle is the biggest depositor; and the meanest.

Kate Beringer and Billy work side by side as tellers.

Billy is puzzled when five Mogwais seal themselves up in sticky cocoons.

What come out
of the cocoons
are gremlins.

The gremlins
waste no time
in attacking
Billy's mother
and leaving
a trail of
devastation
all over town.

To escape from deadly daylight, the gremlins
take shelter in the movie theater.

Billy blows the theater up.
But the devilish gremlins
aren't finished yet.

With Gizmo's help, Billy and Kate succeed in putting
an end to the nightmarish menace of the gremlins.

Billy turned the corner and saw Stripe. The gremlin was playing with some of the toys.

Stripe sent a large toy bird flying at Billy's face. Billy was knocked off balance. By the time he recovered, Stripe was gone.

HEE HEE HEE

Billy wandered into the T.V. department. Suddenly Stripe's evil face appeared on every T.V. in the store!

Billy ran to the video cameras hoping to catch the gremlin. Stripe was waiting with a bow and arrow, aimed right at Billy!

Suddenly the store's bright lights came on. Stripe dropped his weapon and ran, screaming in pain. He was searching for someplace that was still dark.

Kate had found the store's control center, and had turned on the lights from there.

Kate flipped all the switches she could find.

Meanwhile, Stripe
had come upon the
store's greenhouse.
There were no lights
in here, and the
windows had been
covered with heavy
canvas. It was dark
here, a good place for
him to rest.

The greenhouse fountain suddenly came on. Stripe grinned wickedly when he
saw the steady flow of water. When water touched a gremlin, he multiplied
into many gremlins!

Stripe splashed and danced happily in the fountain. As his body got wet, small blisters began to form on his skin. These would pop off and become other gremlins. In a few seconds there would be hundreds of gremlins once again!

Billy saw Stripe in the fountain, and ran back to Kate.

Kate! You turned on the fountain! Turn it off!

I don't know which switch it is!

GIZMO!

Gizmo also saw Stripe. He hopped into a toy car and rushed toward the greenhouse.

As soon as Gizmo got to the greenhouse, he leaped from the car and started to untie the rope that held the canvas in place.

Gizmo struggled with the rope, for several agonizing minutes. Finally he got the knot loose.

The canvas fell from the windows, flooding the greenhouse with sunlight. The bright, warm rays were too much for Stripe. He disappeared in a puff of smoke, gone forever. Gizmo, still holding the rope, dangled high in the air. Billy and Kate rushed over and helped him down.

"Gizmo, you did it!" said Kate, as they headed home.

"Way to go, buddy!" said Billy.

Gizmo smiled.

The nightmare was over. This time, the gremlins were gone for good.

ABC

The Alef-Bet Book
The Israel Museum, Jerusalem

Florence Cassen Mayers

Harry N. Abrams, Inc.
Publishers
New York
and
The Domino Press
Jerusalem

For my mother, Marie Cassen

Editor: Harriet Whelchel
Designer: Florence Cassen Mayers
Picture Research: Irène Lewitt, Genya Markon, The Israel Museum

Library of Congress Cataloging-in-Publication Data
Mayers, Florence Cassen.
ABC: the alef-bet book: the Israel Museum, Jerusalem / by
Florence Cassen Mayers; introduction by Martin Weyl.
p. cm.
English and Hebrew.
Summary: Presents the Hebrew alphabet, using each letter to introduce
the Israeli art, Judaica, ethnography and archaeological collections at the Israel
Museum.
ISBN 0-8109-1885-4
1. Hebrew language—Alphabet—Juvenile literature. 2. Art, Israeli—Juvenile
literature. 3. Israel—Antiquities—Juvenile literature. [1. Hebrew language—
Alphabet. 2. Israel Museum (Jerusalem). 3. Art, Israeli. 4. Israel—Antiquities.
5. Museums. 6. Alphabet.] I. Muze'on Yiśra'el (Jerusalem). II. Title.
PJ4589. M39 1989
492.4'11—dc 19
88-27501

The photographers are: Moshe Caine, Avi Ganor, David Harris, Yoram
Lehmann, Nachum Slapak

Objects credited to IDAM are reproduced by courtesy of the Israel
Department of Antiquities and Museums

Object for 'Gimel' is reproduced by courtesy of the artist's representative
© Daniel Doron Tel-Aviv

Printed and bound in Japan

Other Books in the ABC Series
ABC: Museum of Fine Arts, Boston
ABC: The Museum of Modern Art, New York
ABC: The National Air and Space Museum
ABC: Egyptian Art from The Brooklyn Museum
ABC: Costume and Textiles from the Los Angeles County Museum of Art
ABC: Musical Instruments from The Metropolitan Museum of Art

Isaiah Scroll   מגילת ישעיהו הגדולה
Book of Isaiah, 3:24–7:15   (ג': כ"ד – ז': ט"ו)
Qumran Caves, c. 100 BC   מערות קומראן, 100 לפסה"נ בקירוב
Parchment, 10½" × 24'4"   קלף, 734×26.2 ס"מ (כל המגילה)
Dead Sea Scrolls,   המגילות הגנוזות
Shrine of the Book   היכל הספר

Introduction

In this creative new bilingual ABC book, preschoolers and beginning readers are provided a captivating initiation into the alphabet—*alef-bet*—of the Hebrew language. From *alef* (represented by *arayot,* or lions) to *tav* (*takhshitim,* or jewelry), the *alef-bet* is illuminated through beautiful images that draw from the rich diversity of the culture of Israel.

There is no more appropriate source for these images than The Israel Museum, a multi-unit complex that has served as the national museum of Israel since 1965. Included in this ABC are artifacts and art from the five major units of the museum. From the museum's Shrine of the Book come the Dead Sea Scrolls, the oldest biblical manuscripts in the world. The archaeological collections offer a delicate limestone mask from the seventh millennium BC, colorful beads from the seventh–fifth century BC, and a Byzantine mosaic floor panel. While the fine-art collections cover a broad range—from Far Eastern art and Old Master paintings to Impressionist and Post-Impressionist and twentieth-century art—this book focuses on the museum's collections of ethnic artifacts, Judaica, and Israeli art. Pictured are a silver Torah pointer, exotic jewelry, and paintings by contemporary Israeli artists. Complementing those paintings are examples of contemporary sculpture from the Isamu Noguchi–designed sculpture garden. The youth wing is represented by a charming view of Jerusalem from the special exhibition *Children of the World Paint Jerusalem.* These and the many other pieces shown will intrigue and delight children of all ages.

As befits a national institution, The Israel Museum maintains restoration and research facilities and a special department that sends traveling exhibitions to schools, community centers, and local museums throughout Israel. It is the privilege of this *alef-bet* book to serve as a special adjunct to these programs.

Martin Weyl, Director
The Israel Museum

Note: Hebrew is read from right to left, and a Hebrew book opens from left to right. Therefore, to begin this book, turn it over. Then lift the cover and you will soon find the first Hebrew letter, *alef.*

The Hebrew words are transliterated (spelled in English characters), to show how they are pronounced, and also translated, to show what they mean.

Title page:
Menashe Kadishman, Israel (b. 1932)
Suspense, 1966
Painted iron, 10²⁄₃″ × 7′7¼″ × 15½″
Gift of the artist with the assistance of Mrs. A. Sacher, London, 1966

דף שער:
מנשה קדישמן, ישראל (נ. 1932)
מתח, 1966
ברזל צבוע, 39×228×302 ס״מ
מתנת האמן בסיוע הגב׳ א. סאקר
לונדון, 1966

Tav

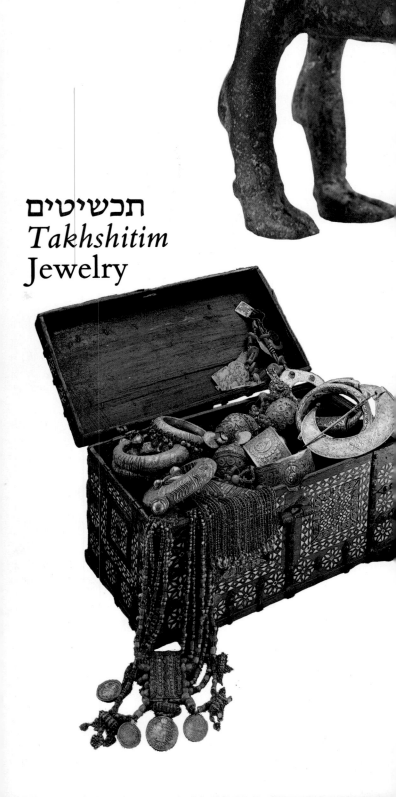

תכשיטים
Takhshitim
Jewelry

Shin שׁ

שׁוֹר
Shor
Bull

Bull statuette   פסלון של שור
Northwest Samaria,   צפון־מערב השומרון
12th century BC   המאה הי"ב לפסה"נ
Bronze, height 5″   ברונזה, גובה 12.5 ס"מ
Archaeological Staff Office,   מאוספי קמ"ט ארכיאולוגיה,
Judea and Samaria   יהודה ושומרון

Yemenite jewelry box with   קופסת תכשיטים תימנית ובה תכשיטים
jewelry from Yemen, Morocco,   מתימן, מרוקו וטוניס
and Tunisia, 20th century   המאה הכ'
Box: wood inlaid with   הקופסה: עץ משובץ צדף
mother-of-pearl, 14 × 17½ × 13½″   34×44×35 ס"מ
Jewelry: silver, coral beads,   התכשיטים: כסף, חרוזי אלמוג ואמייל
and enamel   קופסה: אוסף ראתיינס
Box: Rathjens Collection   השאלה קבועה,
Permanent Loan, Zalman Schocken   זלמן שוקן

רקמה
Rikma
Embroidery

Resh

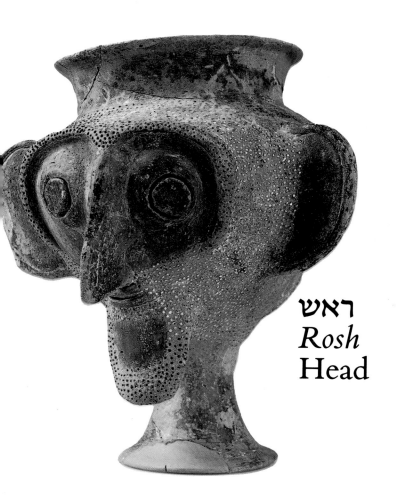

ראש
Rosh
Head

קערה
Ke'ara
Bowl

Teapot
Morocco, 20th century
Silver-plated brass, height 8″
Gift of Baroness Alix de Rothschild

ומקום
זוקו, המאה הכ'
ליז מצופה כסף, גובה 20 ס"מ
תנת הברונית אליקס דה־רוטשילד

Koof

קומקום
Kumkum
Teapot

Bowl
Provenance unknown,
2nd–1st century BC
Mold-made glass,
height 2½″, diameter 4″
Gift of Binyanei Ha'uma, Jerusalem

קערה
מקור בלתי ידוע
המאה הב'-הא' לפסה"נ
זכוכית עשויה על גבי תבנית
גובה 6.3 ס"מ, קוטר 10 ס"מ
מתנת בניני האומה, ירושלים

צלחת
Tzalakhat
Plate

צעצוע
Tza'atzua
Toy

Purim plate
France, 18th century
Painted faience, diameter 9″
Gift in memory of Raphael and
Hannah Sidi, Paris

Shmuel Kaplan, Israel (b. 1944)
Trailer truck, 1979
Solid wood, 2½ × 7⅔ × 1¼″
Gift of the designer

לחת למשלוח מנות
רפת, המאה הי״ח
איאנס צבוע, קוטר 22.5 ס״מ
תנה לזכר רפאל
חנה סידי, פריס

מואל קפלן, ישראל (נ. 1944)
שאית־גרר, (1979)
ץ, 3×19.5×6.5 ס״מ
תנת המעצב

Tzadi

צִיפּוֹר
Tzipor
Bird

Spice box in shape of bird
Poland, late 18th century
Silver, height 11⅔"

הדס בשמים בצורת ציפור
פולין, סוף המאה הי"ח
כסף, גובה 29.5 ס"מ

פסיפס
Pseyfas
Mosaic

Mosaic floor panels
Church at Kissufim, Negev,
6th century
Stone and glass, 60⅔ × 63″
IDAM

רצפת פסיפס
כנסייה, כיסופים בנגב
המאה הו' לסה"נ
אבן וזכוכית, 160×154.5 ס"מ
מאוספי אגף העתיקות

Ayin

עצים
Etzim
Trees

Israel Paldi, Israel (1892–1979)
Israel Landscape, 1928
Oil on canvas, 25¼ × 29¼″
Purchase, Batsheva de Rothschild
Fund, 1963

ישראל פלדי, ישראל (1892-1979)
נוף ישראלי, 1928
שמן על בד, 73×63 ס"מ
רכישת קרן בת־שבע
דה־רוטשילד, 1963

ספר
Sefer
Book

De Castro Pentateuch	חומש דה־קאסטרו
Germany, 1344	גרמניה, 1344
Illuminated manuscript on vellum	כתב־יד מעוטר על קלף
Binding of Pentateuch:	כריכת החומש:
Amsterdam, 1647	אמסטרדם, 1647
Gold-tooled leather	עור מוטבע בזהב
with engraved brass clasps,	ואבזמי פליז חקוקים
18⅓ × 12⅓" closed	31×46 ס״מ סגור
Acquired with the advice of	נרכש בעצת
Joseph and Caroline Gruss,	ג'וזף וקרולין גרוס
and with the assistance of	ובסיוע אגודת
Friends of The Israel Museum	ידידי מוזיאון ישראל

Nun ‎נ

‎נגנים
Naganim
Musicians

Musicians
Scroll of Esther (detail)
Holland, 18th century
Parchment, 9⅔″ × 9′9½″

‎נגנים
‎מגילת אסתר (פרט)
‎הולנד, המאה הי״ח
‎קלף, ×24.5×294 ס״מ

מסכה
Masekha
Mask

Mask
Nahal Hemar Cave,
Dead Sea region,
7th millennium BC
Limestone, 10⅓ × 6⅔″
IDAM

Mem

מסכה
מערת נחל חמר,
איזור ים המלח
האלף השביעי לפסה"נ
אבן, 26×17 ס"מ
מאוספי אגף העתיקות

Lamed

ליצן
Leytzan
Clown

Issachar Ber Ryback,
Russia (1897–1953)
The Jester, c. 1923–25
Gouache on paper, 25½ × 18″
Lent by Y. Einhorn

ששכר בר ריבק
רוסיה (1897-1953)
ליצן, 1923-1925 בקירוב
אש על נייר, 64×45 ס"מ
שאלת י. איינהורן

כ
Kaf

כיפות
Kippot
Caps

Man's cap	כיפה של גבר
Afghanistan, 20th century	אפגאניסטאן, המאה הכ'
Embroidered cotton,	כותנה רקומה
height 8″, diameter 7½″	גובה 20 ס"מ, קוטר 19 ס"מ
Man's cap	כיפה של גבר
Buchara, 20th century	בוכרה, המאה הכ'
Gold and silver-thread embroidery	רקמת חוטי זהב וכסף
on red and green velvet,	על קטיפה אדומה וירוקה
height 2⅓″, diameter 7¼″	גובה 6 ס"מ, קוטר 18 ס"מ
Man's cap	כיפה של גבר
Buchara, 20th century	בוכרה, המאה הכ'
Multicolored cotton-thread embroidery,	רקמת חוטי כותנה צבעוניים
height 6⅓″, diameter 7½″	גובה 16 ס"מ, קוטר 19 ס"מ
Gift of Baroness Alix de Rothschild	מתנת הברונית אליקס דה-רוטשילד

Yod

יד לתורה
Yad L'Torah
Torah pointer

Torah pointer
Poland, 1855
Silver, cast, cut, engraved,
pierced, and filigree
length 11½″, diameter 1⅔″
Stieglitz Collection
Donated with the contribution
of Erica and Ludwig Jesselson,
through American Friends
of the Israel Museum

ד לתורה
ולין, 1855
סף יצוק, גזור וחקוק
יליגראן
ורך 29 ס״מ, קוטר 4.5 ס״מ
וסף שטיגליץ
תן בעזרת תרומה של
ריקה ולודביג יסלזון
אמצעות ידידי המוזיאון
ארה״ב

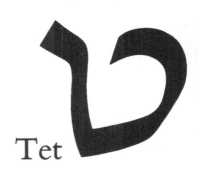

ט

Tet

טלית
Talit
Prayer shawl

Prayer shawl
Italy, late 18th century
Silk, gold-thread embroidery,
74⅓ × 46⅓″
Gift of Jakob Michael in memory
of his wife, Erna Michael, New York

טלית
איטליה, סוף המאה הי״ח
משי רקום בחוטי זהב
186×116 ס״מ
מתנת מר יעקב מיכאל לזכר אשתו,
ארנה מיכאל, ניו־יורק

Khet

חרוזים
Kharuzim
Beads

Beads
Burial Caves at Ketef Hinnom,
Jerusalem, 7th–5th century BC
Carnelian, glass, agate, silver
IDAM

חרוזים
ממערות קבורה בכתף־הינונם,
ירושלים, המאה הז'־הה' לפסה"נ
קרניאול, זכוכית, אגאט, כסף
מאוספי אגף העתיקות

Zayin ז

זוג
Zug
Couple

Male and female figurines
Beersheba region,
4th millennium BC
Ivory
Male: height 13¼″, IDAM
Female: height 11½″, Gift of
Mrs. Sarah Solomon, Haifa

פסלונים של גבר ואשה
אזור באר־שבע
האלף הרביעי לפסה״נ
שנהב
גבר: 33 ס״מ, מאוספי אגף העתיקות
אשה: 29 ס״מ, מתנת גב׳ שרה סלומון,
חיפה

Vav

וו
Vav
Hook

Hook
Nahal Hemar Cave, Dead Sea region,
7th millennium BC
Bone, 3⅞ × 1⅓″
IDAM

וו
מערת נחל חמר, אזור ים המלח
האלף השביעי לפסה"נ
עצם, 3.3×8.24 ס"מ
מאוספי אגף העתיקות

Heh

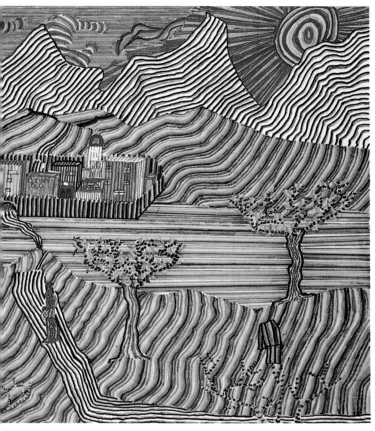

הרים
Harim
Hills

Hills in Jerusalem
Executed for exhibition
Children of the World
Paint Jerusalem, 1977
Deborah Terracina,
13 years old, Italy
Crayon on paper, 12 × 18″

הרים בירושלים
ציור לתערוכה 'ילדי העולם
מציירים את ירושלים', 1977
דבורה טרצ'ינה,
בת 13, איטליה
עפרון על נייר, 45×30 ס"מ

ים דמויי דג
'מעלה: תל אל־עג'ול,
נמאה הט"ז לפסה"נ
נהט, אורך 15 ס"מ
האוספי אגף העתיקות
מטה: תל פולג,
נמאה הי"ט לפסה"נ
ורס, אורך 19 ס"מ

דגים
Dagim
Fish

Fish-shaped vessels
Above: Tel-el-Ajjul,
16th century BC
Alabaster, length 6″
IDAM
Below: Tel Poleg,
19th century BC
Pottery, length 7½″

גמל
Gamal
Camel

Shalom Moskovitz (Shalom of Safed),
Israel (1887–1980)
Abraham and Lot (with detail)
Gouache on paper, 18¼ × 24½"
Gift of Jean Aberbach through the
America-Israel Cultural Foundation

שלום מוסקוביץ (שלום מצפת),
ישראל (1980-1887)
אברהם ולוט
גואש על נייר, 61.5×45.5 ס"מ
מתנת מר ג'ין אברבוך
באמצעות קרן תרבות אמריקה-ישראל

Bet

בקבוק
Bakbuk
Bottle

Wine Bottle for Kiddush
Inscription: Blessing over the wine
for Sabbath
(Book of Genesis, 1:31−2:1)
Syria, 19th century
Etched red glass, 6⅞ × 4⅔″
Gift through Jakob Michael,
New York, 1968

בקבוק יין לקידוש
כתובת קידוש על היין
ליום השבת
בראשית: א': ל"ג עד ב': א')
סוריה, המאה הי"ט
זכוכית צרובה, 17×12 ס"מ
מתנה באמצעות יעקב מיכאל,
ניו-יורק, 1968

Alef א

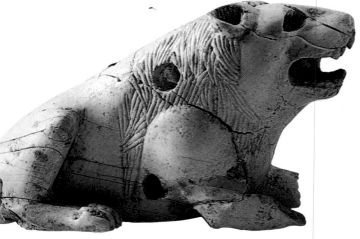

אריות
Arayot
Lions

Two crouching lions
Samaria, 9th–8th century BC
Ivory, height 1⅝″
IDAM

אריות קורסים
שומרון, המאה הט'-הח' לפסה"נ
שנהב, גובה 4 ס"מ
מאוספי אגף העתיקות

הקדמה

ספר דו-לשוני חדש זה מציע לילדים בגיל הרך ולקוראים
מתחילים הזדמנות להכיר היכרות ראשונה את *האלף-בית* של
השפה העברית.

החל באלף (אריות) וכלה בתו (תכשיטים) – אותיות
האלף-בית מיוצגות בחפצי אמנות הלקוחים מן התרבות
הישראלית המגוונת והעשירה.

מוזיאון ישראל הוא מרכז חשוב ביותר למוצגי אמנות אלה,
ומאז 1965 הוא המוזיאון הלאומי של ישראל.

בספר *האלף-בית* כלולים מוצגים וחפצי אמנות מחמשת
האגפים העיקריים של המוזיאון: מהיכל הספר – המגילות
הגנוזות, שהן כתבי-היד התנ״כיים העתיקים ביותר בעולם; מן
האוסף הארכיאולוגי – מסכת אבן עדינה מן האלף השביעי
לפסה״נ; חרוזים צבעוניים מן המאות הה׳-הז׳ לפסה״נ, ורצפת
פסיפס ביזנטית. אוספי האמנות היפה כוללים מגוון רחב – החל
באמנות המזרח הרחוק וציורי אמני המופת, ועד לאמנות
האימפרסיוניסטית, הפוסט-אימפרסיוניסטית והאמנות בת-זמננו
– ואילו ספר זה מתמקד באמנות אתנית, אמנות יהודית ואמנות
ישראלית: יד לתורה עשויה כסף, מעשי רקמה ותכשיטים
אקזוטיים, תמונות של אמנים ישראליים בני-זמננו ופסלים
מודרניים המוצבים בגן-הפסלים שעוצב בידי איסאמו נוגוצ׳י.
אגף הנוער מיוצג בתמונות נוף של ירושלים, מתוך התערוכה
הייחודית *ילדי העולם מציירים את ירושלים* (1977).

כל אלה, ומוצגים רבים אחרים, יעוררו עניין והנאה בקרב
ילדים בני כל הגילים.

במוזיאון ישראל קיימות מעבדות לשימור ושחזור, ומחלקה
מיוחדת המניידת תערוכות לבתי-ספר, מרכזים קהילתיים
ומוזיאונים אחרים ברחבי הארץ.

ספר *האלף-בית* יעשיר תכניות אלה.

מרטין וייל, מנכ״ל
מוזיאון ישראל

Deuteronomy Scroll   מגילת ספר דברים
Fragment including   קטע המכיל את עשרת הדברות
Ten Commandments   מערות קומראן, 30-1 לפסה״נ בקירוב
Qumran Caves, c. 30–1 BC   קלף, 9.6×95 ס״מ (כל המגילה)
Parchment, 3¾ × 38″   המגילות הגנוזות
Dead Sea Scrolls,   היכל הספר
Shrine of the Book

לאמי, מרי קאסן

עריכה: הרייט וולצ׳ל
עיצוב: פלורנס קאסן מאיירס
מחקר תמונות: אירן לויט, גניה מרקון, מוזיאון ישראל

יצא לאור ב־1989 ע״י הארי נ. אברמס, ניו־יורק
בשיתוף הוצאת ספרים דומינו, ירושלים.

תמונת הגמל המציין את האות "ג׳" באדיבות נציג האמן
© דניאל דורון, תל־אביב

Printed and bound in Japan

צלמים: משה קן, אבי גנור, דוד הריס, יורם להמן, נחום סלפק

Title page:
Michael Gross, Israel (b. 1920)
Queen, 1969–70
Painted steel, height 11′8″, diameter 24″
Purchase, Riklis Fund, 1971

דף שער:
מיכאל גרוס, ישראל (נ. 1920)
מלכה, 1969-1970
פלדה צבועה
גובה 350 ס״מ, קוטר 60 ס״מ
רכישת קרן ריקליס, 1971

אבג

ספר האלף־בית
מוזיאון ישראל, ירושלים

פלורנס קאסן מאיירס

האריי נ. אברמס
מוציאים לאור
ניו־יורק
והוצאת ספרים דומינו
ירושלים